Northumberlan

GW00383641

on old picture p

George Na....

THE HARTLEY CATASTROPHE.

16 January 1862.
204 lives lost.

1. This artist's impression of the Hartley pit disaster is from an engraving depicting one of the worst-ever mining accidents. On Thursday 16th January 1862, the beam over the shaft, weighing 43 tons, snapped in two, half of it crashing down the shaft. A cage was ascending at the time, and it seems miraculous that three of its occupants survived. There was only the one shaft, so rescuing any survivors was nearly impossible. Miners from the surrounding area rushed to the scene, and worked for six days and nights to clear it. Time and again they were beaten back by choke-damp. Not until the Wednesday did they finally succeed in reaching the seam. The bodies of the 204 men and boys (and 43 ponies) were found lying in rows, all quiet and placid. After this catastrophe, all pits had to have a second shaft. The postcard featuring the engraving was published c.1906

Designed and published by Reflections of a Bygone Age, Keyworth, Nottingham 2018

Printed by Adlard Print and Typesetting Services, Ruddington, Notts.

Introduction

The Northumberland coalfield is the northern half of the Great Northern Coalfield, stretching from the Scottish border to North Yorkshire. From the Pennines in the west of the county with its many drift mines to the larger, deeper seams towards the North sea coast, the area was rich in coal. The most productive pits were in the east of the county, including Ellington, Lynemouth and Ashington.

Northumberland has had a lot open-cast mining over the years, especially to the east of the Great North Road, and this is the only output of coal from the county today.

Transporting coal in the early days was by means of wagonways laid with wooden rails to carry horse-drawn wagons to staithes for loading onto collier boats. The main ports were Amble, Blyth and Newcastle. Northumberland was principally an exporting coalfield and was thus more susceptible to the ups and downs of world trade.

Although picture postcards were introduced in Britain in 1894, it was only in 1902 when the Post Office relaxed their rules to allow the message to be written on the same side as the address that their use really took off. The period from then until the end of the First World War really was the Golden Age of picture postcards, with millions posted daily, their use being the equivalent to email, facebook or text message in today's society. Postcards posted in the morning could be delivered the same day if posted to an address in the same town.

Picture postcards were at the height of their popularity in the 1900-18 period, during which time they were used because people did not have telephones - or access to photographs of newsworthy events or personalities of the day - to send messages to friends or relatives (" *I will be arriving tomorrow by the 1.20 train"*) or show them what was going on in the sender's neighbourhood. Local views enabled people to send pictures of streets and buildings, and an added bonus was that until 1918 postcards could be posted for one halfpenny, half the letter rate. Cards were avidly collected and housed in specially-made albums, filled with examples received from friends or postcards bought from the local shop. In this period, the North-East of England had some excellent firms who published cards - Auty of Tynemouth (one of the earliest postcard publishers in Britain), Gibson and Johnston of Gateshead, and Collier of Bellingham, along with many others based in small towns and villages. Together they provided an amazing portfolio of photographic postcards that depicted the mining industry in Northumberland in the early part of the 20th century. Details of publishers are provided where known.

It may seem strange to us today that cards were published showing disasters, but these were fulfilling the role of today's TV or newspaper pictures. The Barnsley firm of Warner Gothard specialised in these, producing commemorative disaster and event postcards from Northumberland to Hampshire and Somerset, including some Durham coal mining examples - two of the Glebe Colliery explosion of February 1908, and three of the West Stanley disaster a year later.

The Durham equivalent of this book, published in 2016, shows a few of the large number of disaster cards produced for that county. The only contemporary postcard I've seen for Northumberland (in my 40 years of collecting postcards!) is one for the 1925 Montague disaster. The Hartley disaster of 1862 appeared on a postcard almost half a century after the event.

After 1918, the popularity of postcards fell sharply, and instead of a range of cards portraying a multiplicity of images, viewcards and seaside comics formed the bulk of postcard output. The doubling of the postage rate for cards, increased use of the telephone and more photographic content in newspapers all diminished the use of postcards to show local events. Some continued to be featured on cards, but these are much harder to find.

The last deep mine producing coal in the county, at Ellington, closed in 2005, bringing to an end hundreds of years of coal working in Northumberland. The only colliery left standing is at Woodhorn, near Ashington, where a museum and archives allow visitors to take in exhibitions and see the historic buildings.

George Nairn
June 2018

Hartley Memorial and Church, Earsdon.

2. St. Alban's Church, Earsdon, and the Hartley Colliery disaster memorial. On 26th January 1862, the funeral procession stretched from Hartley to Earsdon, some four miles. The reaction from the public, and from Queen Victoria, maintained the story in the press for over a month. This postcard was posted to Walsall in May 1916.

New Pit, Hartley.

3. A c.1904 picture postcard by uncredited publisher of New Hartley Colliery, owned by Hartley Main Collieries Ltd.

4. A view of the Scremerston Colliery road locomotive and trailer, with the colliery in the background. This was one of the most northerly collieries in Northumberland. The postcard, from a Glasgow publisher, was posted at Berwick in August 1904.

5. This postcard from one of the area's leading publishers, Auty of Tynemouth, shows the deputy miners' houses at Scremerston Colliery. A horse and cart is loading coal from rail trucks to deliver 'land sale' coal around the local houses. The steam wagon appears to have a load of new timber. Card posted at Cornhill-on-Tweed in September 1907.

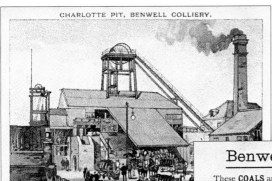

CHARLOTTE PIT, BENWELL COLLIERY.

6. A c.1908 promotional item rather than a postcard, this artist-drawn scene of Benwell Colliery's Charlotte Pit advertises the then current prices for Benwell coal.

Benwell Best House Coals.

These **COALS** are supplied direct from the Colliery to consumers, at the under-noted prices, delivered free to any part of Newcastle (Gosforth, Byker, and Heaton, 1/- extra) :—

	PER 15 CWT.	PER TON.		PER 15 CWT.	PER TON
Best Screened -	11/6	**14/6**	Rough Small -	**9/9**	**11/6**
Seconds ,,	- 11/3	**14/3**	Beaumont Best		
Thirds ,,	- 11/-	**14/-**	Screened -	**12/9**	**16/-**
Nuts ,,	- 10/6	**13/-**			

Daily deliveries of Coal in Bags.

I am also prepared (to suit customers that have not accommodation for Cart Loads) to deliver **BEST SCREENED** at

5d..

per half-cwt. bag, by my waggons as they pass your doors.

TERMS–CASH ON DELIVERY.

WEIGHT GUARANTEED.

THESE COALS ARE CLEAN, DARK ASH, DURABLE, AND PRODUCE A GREAT HEAT. YOUR ORDERS WILL BE ESTEEMED AND HAVE PROMPT ATTENTION.

Charlotte Pit, Benwell Colliery, January, 1905.   WILLIAM COCHRAN CARR.

TEAR OFF HERE AND KEEP PICTURE.

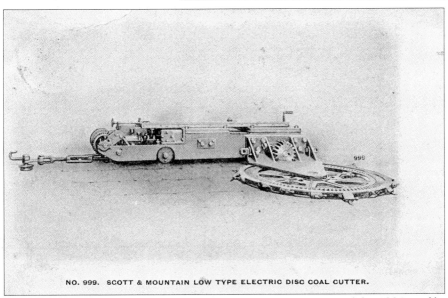

NO. 999. SCOTT & MOUNTAIN LOW TYPE ELECTRIC DISC COAL CUTTER.

7. A rare postcard, showing early mining machinery, posted in 1904 to New Shildon. Ernest Scott & Mountain Ltd was established in Newcastle-upon-Tyne in 1890 and acquired by C.A. Parsons and Co. of Heaton in 1913. The postcard was published by Thomson & Lee of Newcastle.

SHILBOTTLE COLLIERY.

8. The Co-operative Wholesale Society bought Shilbottle Colliery in 1917 from Shilbottle Coal Co. Ltd. It had a two-mile rail connection to the main Newcastle to Edinburgh line just south of Alnmouth station. Shilbottle coals were acknowledged to be the best house coals produced for durability, heat and freedom from ash. This postcard was published by the company as an advertising and correspondence card.

The Colliery, Longframlington.

9. When this postcard was published c.1905 the owners of Longframlington Colliery were the Shilbottle Coal Co. In 1917 the CWS took over. The coal was carried via an overhead ropeway crossing the A1 road to the screening plant at Whittle Colliery. Longframlington Colliery closed on the last day of 1931.

10. Creswell Colliery band was formed in 1899. This postcard shows the trophies won at the British Open Championships in 1925 at Belle Vue, Manchester. The band's conductor at the time was J.A. Greenwood.

11. The Amble sword-dancing team c.1923. This form of two-handled sword dance was popular with Northumberland and Durham miners. It was based around Amble, Bedlington, Earsdon, Monkseaton, Newbiggin, Prudhoe, Mickley, Walbottle and Westerhope.

12. A rare postcard showing Bullock's Hall Coal Company's miners working under police protection. It was published by photographer J.A. Pringle of Amble. The colliery was owned in the early 20th century by the above company and in the 1920s by T.W. Watkin and R.G. Hudson. It closed in 1933.

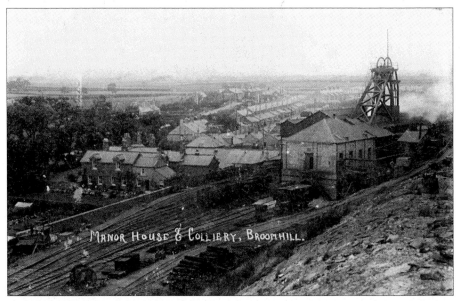

13. Broomhill Colliery and village on a postcard by unknown publisher. It produced steam and household coals, which were conveyed to Broomhill Quay staithes at Amble. The colliery closed in 1961.

The Harbour, Amble. 1870

14. Amble harbour on a 'Monarch' series postcard published by R. Johnston of Gateshead, many of whose postcards feature in this book, and posted at Amble in August 1939. The photo shows colliers being loaded at Broomhill staithes. These ceased working in the 1960s and the staithes were demolished.

FENNEY BED COLLIERY. 1909.

15. Fenney Bed Colliery during its construction in 1909, seen on a postcard published by Pringle of Amble. The colliery was owned by the Widdrington Coal Co. and made its first shipment of coals to Amble in September 1910. Its life was short, though, the colliery closing in 1924. An application was made in 2016 to re-open it!

16. Broomhill Colliery band outside the 'Grey's Arms Hotel' at Redrow in 1906. They featured in competitions from the 1890s and were regulars at the Northumberland Miners' Gala. This postcard was sent from Amble to South Broomhill in June 1907.

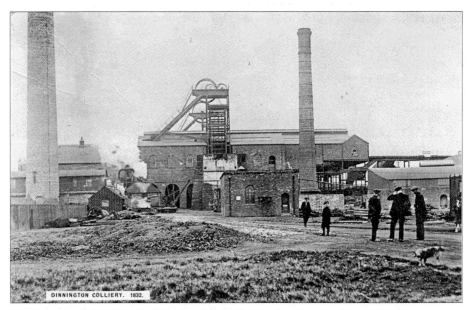

17. Dinnington Colliery lay five miles north-west of Newcastle and is featured here on another fine Johnston-published card. It closed on 26th February 1960.

Modern Screening Plant, Cambois Colliery

18. An anonymously-published photographic postcard of Cambois Colliery near Blyth, showing the new coal screening plant and plenty of pit props in the yard. The colliery closed on 20th April 1968.

A PIT. SLEEKBURN. 1287.

19. Another Johnston postcard (all were meticulously numbered) of Sleekburn 'A' pit. It was posted at Bedlington Colliery in January 1929, sent to Newsham, Northumberland.

20. Settlingstone Colliery, originally a lead mine in the 19th century, was about three miles north-west of Newbrough. It had an unusual 1ft 7in. gauge endless rope tramway. Card published by Collier of Bellingham.

21. The local constabulary escort strike-breakers during the Settlingstone strike, while some miners with bicycles look on.

22. This early solid-tyred vehicle was owned by Settlingstones Mines Ltd and is pictured on this postcard at Fourstones. Published by Elliott Brothers of Hexham, the card was posted at Fourstones in June 1914.

23. Thirlwall Colliery was situated three-quarters of a mile east of Gilsland station on the Newcastle-Carlisle railway line. It had a tramway running down the hillside to the screens and sidings. The colliery closed in 1926.

24. The Tynedale Coal Company used this postcard as an advertising medium. On the reverse it states that the company *" will be pleased to quote you for 4 or 5 tons of their household coals, delivered by motor waggon on application"*. This view shows Acomb Colliery, which by 1919 was owned by Acomb Coal Co., a subsidiary of Mickey Coal Co. The card was posted at Hexham in October 1906.

AGED MINERS' HOMES, WOODHORN. 1718.

25. The Northumberland Aged Miners' Homes Association was established in 1900 to help retired miners find accomodation when evicted from their colliery homes. The first few of them were built at East Chevington in 1902, but this Johnston-published postcard shows homes at Woodhorn.

26. A postcard published by Valentine of Dundee, one of the leading British picture postcard firms in the first two-thirds of the 20th century. It shows Hartford House near Bedlington, built in 1811 for William Burrow. In May 1944 it became a miners' rehabilitation centre. The card was posted in 1936.

27. This superb postcard view shows the back of Doctor Terrace in Bedlington, a typical mining street. The houses were built in 1874. To the right can be seen rain butts and on the left coal houses and 'netties' (earth closets). Residents would have had to contend with a 'clarty' (muddy) road!

28. The shafts for the colliery at Newbiggin were sunk in 1908. This 'Monarch' series postcard from R. Johnston of Gateshead was probably published soon after this. It was posted in 1915. The colliery closed on 11th November 1967.

29. 'Kit', an 0-6-0 saddle tank, built by the Yorkshire Engine Co. of Sheffield in 1910 with the works number 1022, is pictured at Newbiggin Colliery.

30. This postcard shows a pit pony with its tub and admirers after winning first prize in a show near Newbiggin.

31. The harbour at Blyth on a Valentine-published postcard posted at Blyth in May 1908. To the right can be seen the Blyth Steam Tug Company's vessel *Earl of Beaconsfield*, built by J.P. Rennoldson of South Shields in 1877. It was used to assist collier ships in and out of the narrow harbour.

DOCTOR PIT BEDLINGTON

32. This picture epitomises the appeal and cultural significance of old postcards in p shows a scene at Doctor Pit, Bedlington, opened in the 1850s. Note the buffers on th closed in March 1962.

nique photographic source material. This one, from an uncredited publisher c.1906,
ddle tank for use while shunting various types of trucks and chaldrons. The colliery

33. A Johnston-published postcard of Ellington Colliery. Sunk in 1909, it was to become one of the north-east's largest collieries, known locally as 'the big E'. In 1986, around 2,170 men produced 45,000 tonnes of coal each week. The mine was closed by British Coal in February 1994. Shortly afterwards it was re-opened by a private company, but with recurring water problems it finally closed in 2005, the last colliery in the north-east.

34. Stobswood Colliery on a postcard by unknown publisher, showing construction work in progress. The colliery opened in 1875 and closed on 1st May 1965.

Woodhorn Colliery. (723)

35. This Johnston-published postcard shows a very busy colliery yard. The Scotch derrick crane was used for loading and offloading rail wagons. Some of the buildings are preserved today and can be visited as part of the Woodhorn Museum and Northumberland Archives. The card was postally used in September 1916.

36. Woodhorn miners pose for this real photographic postcard c.1908. They present a fashion line-up, Edwardian-style, and one in the centre is smoking a clay pipe.

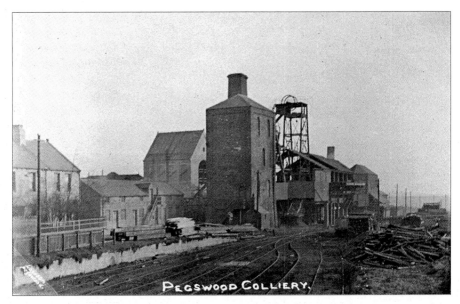

37. Pegswood Colliery lay between Morpeth and Ashington. It opened in 1868 and closed in February 1969. Card published by local photographer Lawson.

38. The Pegswood area yielded good fireclay, so there were extensive brickworks.

39. Linton Colliery was owned by the Ashington Coal Co., being sunk in 1894 and closing on 28th September 1968. This postcard was published by Dundee firm Valentine in their excellent 'X.L.' series.

40. Many surface jobs had to be done at the collieries. This postcard shows a group of Linton Colliery joiners, with a young apprentice in the centre.

41. In 1910 a rescue committee was formed by the Durham and Northumberland coal owners' association under the chairmanship of Colonel W.C. Blackett, and a rescue station was built at Elswick, Newcastle-upon-Tyne, at the corner of Scotswood Road and Hannah Street. This postcard shows the men wearing jumpers with the D.N.C.F.R.B. (Durham and Northumberland Collieries Fire Rescue Brigade) acronym.

42. Elswick Rescue Team displaying some of their equipment that would be used during rescues. They would have been in very close proximity to the Montague Colliery disaster on 30th March 1925 *(see illus. 44)*.

NORTH WALBOTTLE COLLIERY, WESTERHOPE

43. North Walbottle Colliery near Westerhope was opened in 1892 and was under the same ownership - North Walbottle Coal Co. Ltd - until its National Coal Board days from 1947. This card was posted at Newburn in March 1912. The message reads: *" This photo is of a pit north of our place, hoping you like it"*. The colliery closed in 1968.

MONTAGUE PIT
The Scene of the Great Disaster whereby 38 Men and Boys were Entombed.

44. A postcard of Montague Colliery in Scotswood, Newcastle, where on 30th March 1925 methane gas extinguished the lamps, plunging 148 men and boys into darkness. This was followed by millions of gallons of water crashing through the pit. 38 miners never made it to the surface. New pumping equipment was installed, but the last body was not recovered until 19th October.

RESCUE AND FIRE BRIGADE, ASHINGTON. 1796.

45. Durham and Northumberland Collieries Rescue and Fire Brigade at Ashington. Opened in 1913, the same year as its Durham equivalent, the building was of a different design. This postcard by Johnston of Gateshead shows the rescue vehicle and fire engine with the crews posing for the photographer. The card was posted at Bedlington in February 1915.

RESCUE AND FIRE BRIGADE, ASHINGTON. 1803.

46. Another superb Johnston-published postcard of Ashington Rescue Station, with the photo taken on the same day as the previous card. The firemen are posing on their Merryweather fire engine, while the rescue vehicle is just visible on the left.

47. Ashington Coal Co. ran a railway 24 hours a day and seven days a week from Hirst Platform at Ashington to Linton and Ellington collieries. As well as carrying miners, the trains took other passengers. Paper tickets were issued, with a different colour for each day. Card by unidentified publisher.

Fitters' and Electricians' Shops, at Ashington. Owners: Messrs. The Ashington Coal Co., Ltd.
Roofs covered with Turners' Trafford Tiles, by Messrs. Dorman, Long & Co., Ltd.

48. This is an advertising postcard from Turner Brothers' Asbestos Co. Ltd, based at Trafford Park, Manchester. It shows the newly-roofed fitters' and electricians' shop at Ashington.

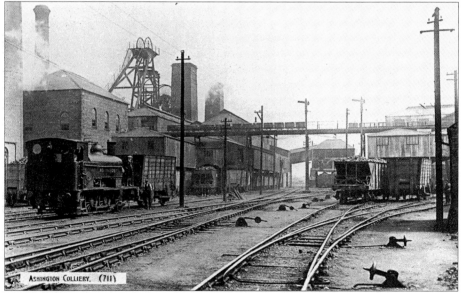

ASHINGTON COLLIERY. (711)

49. Ashington Colliery on a classic Johnston-published 'Monarch' series postcard showing 0-6-0 saddle tank locomotive no. 5 *Ashington* and tubs going along the overhead gantry.

50. The Miners' Theatre and Hall in Station Road, Ashington, opened in 1896. It eventually became the 'Regal' cinema. There was also a miners' literary and debating society, and a Pitman printers' group, along with numerous sports activities. Ashington is the place where many famous footballers were born, including Jackie Milburn and the Charlton brothers.

51. A rare postcard of Howard pit at Netherton, one of the oldest pits in Northumbeland. Sinking took place in 1836 and the mine closed on 4th January 1974. This card was posted at Bedlington in December 1910.

52. Bebside Colliery opened in May 1858, and was owned by the Bebside Coal Co. until April 1925, when it was taken over by Choppington Collieries Ltd. The message on this Johnston-published card, posted to Lowestoft in June 1914 to the senders's mother, read: *" Blyth is a small place no trams all you see is coal dust in the streets and they shoot the coal against back gate the miners have the coal given to them"* (sic.).

53. Local chidren pose at Choppington Colliery for Mr. Johnston to take their photo in front of the coal drops.

54. A card produced by an amateur photographer on postcard-backed paper shows lads putting the coal allocated to miners through coal-holes into coalhouses in a Bedlington back street.

55. Hartley Main Collieries locomotive no. 9, an 0-6-0 tank built in 1921 by R. & W. Hawthorn Leslie of Newcastle. This scene is at Seaton Delaval.

56. Hartley Main Collieries' Seaton Delaval sheds, with six locomotives' tender ends on show.

57. A 'Monarch' series postcard of Seghill Colliery c.1920. In its later life, Seghill comprised The John, The Engine, and Kitty Colliery. It closed on 28th September 1962.

58. Backworth Colliery on a postcard published by Auty, dating from c.1904. The area had good fireclay, so there were extensive brickworks situated there.

Seaton Delaval Colliery

59. A card of Seaton Delaval Colliery, posted at Newcastle in 1905, shows an interesting mixture of railway wagons. The colliery was sunk in 1838 and closed on 27th May 1960.

60. Foster Pit, New Delaval, on a postcard published by T.H. Cosser, stationer, in New Delaval. T.E. Foster invented a method of ventilation using a furnace at the shaft bottom. He was the brother of George Baker Foster, who had led the Hartley Colliery disaster rescue. This colliery closed in April 1955.

61. This postcard, posted in 1921, provides a good view of the chaldron wagons working in the Holywell Colliery sidings.

62. Bluebell Pit at Shiremoor, opened by the Shiremoor Coal Co. in 1874 and closed in 1915. The coal from here was conveyed via the Blyth & Tyne Railway.

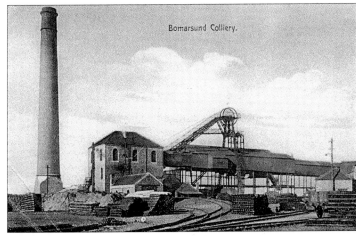

Bomarsund Colliery.

63. Bomarsund Colliery 'F' Pit, near Bedlington, was newly-opened when this postcard was published in 1905 by Graham of Morpeth. The colliery closed in 1965.

64. Northumberland Docks, situated on the Tyne at Howdon, was one of the main loading points for Northumberland coal. Posted from the opposite side of the river at South Shields in 1910, this 'Oswald' series (Newcastle) postcard shows collier ships being loaded at the various coal company staithes.

Northumberland Docks, Howdon on Tyne.   (No. 108)

Telephone: FULham 5225 (5 lines)
Telegrams: Seacoal, Phone, London

Our **FLEET** of **MODERN MOTOR COLLIERS** brings supplies direct from the famous **ASHINGTON COLLIERIES** in **NEWCASTLE**, producing the finest qualities of Coal.
    After being carefully **SCREENED** at **ROSEBANK** Wharf by the most up-to-date plant on the River, deliveries are made by our own transport direct to consumers' cellars.

DELIVERIES TO OUTER SUBURBS AT THESE SPECIAL PRICES DAILY, AFTERNOON.

Urgent orders per Telephone can usually be delivered same day if required.

ORDER CARD

The
Newcastle Coal & Shipping
Co., Ltd.

Rosebank Wharf,

Crab Tree Lane,

FULHAM, S.W.6.

65. An advertising postcard. The reverse quotes 'lowest summer prices', including Newcastle Wallsend at 45 shillings and 6 pence per ton and Newcastle Kitchen coal at 37/6 per ton.

66. The old colliery at Wallsend, seen on a postcard in the 'Lindsey' series, published at 33 Nelson Street, Newcastle, and posted at Wallsend in 1920. It shows the Wallsend 'George' and 'H' pit shafts.

67. A postcard of the new colliery under construction at Wallsend, published by G. Hill. The card was posted in October 1913 to South Wellington, Canada, and part of the message reads: " *Tell the wife that Harriet Rodway was buried today Oct 2. I got this card at Wallsend one night when we were at the baths. I have passed 2 exams for ambulance work*".